THE USBORNE
FAMOUS PAINTINGS
PICTURE BOOK

Megan Cullis

Illustrated by Mark Beech

Designed by Nicola Butler and cover design by Josephine Thompson
Edited by Rosie Dickins and Jane Chisholm
Expert advice by Kathleen Adler

Published in association with the National Gallery Company Ltd.

Contents

Usborne Quicklinks

There are hundreds of famous paintings all over the world. It's impossible to say which are the most famous, as people will always argue about it. To zoom in on famous paintings, take virtual tours of the art galleries and find lots of art activities, go to the Usborne Quicklinks website at www.usborne.com/quicklinks and type in the keywords 'famous paintings sticker book'. Please read our internet safety guidelines on the Usborne Quicklinks website.

Animals

All kinds of animals have featured in paintings,
from famous racehorses to wild and exotic creatures.

This is one of the first times an animal was
painted in such detail. The hare's fur is
picked out with fine, delicate brushstrokes,
so it looks glossy and soft to touch.

If you look closely, you can see the hare's eyelashes,
and even a reflection of a window in its eye.

Young Hare
BY ALBRECHT DÜRER, PAINTED IN 1502

The bird in this picture is a
goldfinch. It was probably
kept as a pet, so its owner
could listen to its beautiful
song. Notice how small
it looks compared
to its perch.

The Goldfinch
BY CAREL FABRITIUS, PAINTED IN 1654

This bold and dramatic
picture was painted
completely from the
artist's imagination.
Henri Rousseau had never
been near a jungle, and
based this scene on sketches
he'd made in parks and
zoos, and things he'd
read in books.

Surprised!
BY HENRI ROUSSEAU,
PAINTED IN 1891

Rousseau based some of these plants
on ornamental houseplants.

According to the artist,
the tiger in the picture was
about to pounce on some
unlucky explorers.

In Japan, carps are a symbol of courage and perseverance. This bold print shows a carp swimming along a stream. Light catches its scales, casting beautiful patterns across its body.

Every year in Japan, families fly carp-shaped kites to celebrate Children's Day. They hope their children will grow up brave and strong, like carp.

Carp in a Stream
BY UTAGAWA HIROSHIGE, MADE IN ABOUT 1838

Whistlejacket was a famous racehorse who lived over 200 years ago. Rearing on his hind legs, he looks strong and powerful. In real life, the painting is almost the size of a real horse.

The artist, George Stubbs, devoted a lot of time to painting horses. He even published a book about horse anatomy, which contained detailed illustrations of horses and their skeletons.

Whistlejacket
BY GEORGE STUBBS, PAINTED IN ABOUT 1762

This picture shows an elephant, horse and cow painted in vibrant colours. The shapes of their bodies seem to blend together, suggesting that they are living in harmony with each other.

Notice how each animal is made up of many blocks of colour.

Elephant, Horse, Cow
BY FRANZ MARC, PAINTED IN 1914

Families

These family portraits reveal a lot about the people they show – not just how they looked, but the relationships between them and the kinds of lives they led.

In the portrait on the right, a wealthy banker, Giovanni Arnolfini, and his wife are standing in their house in Bruges. The couple wear luxurious, fur-trimmed robes, which show off their wealth.

On the wall above the mirror, the artist has signed his name, Jan van Eyck, in Latin.

In the mirror, you can just make out the reflection of some people entering the room. One of them is probably the artist himself.

A dog may have been included in the portrait as a symbol of love and fidelity.

The Arnolfini Portrait
BY JAN VAN EYCK, PAINTED IN 1434

American Gothic
BY GRANT WOOD, PAINTED IN 1930

The artist of this painting, Grant Wood, was inspired by a real house in Iowa, USA, saying that he wanted to show 'the kind of people I fancied should live in that house.' Many people think that the picture shows an American country farmer with his unmarried daughter.

In fact the man was a local dentist. Wood persuaded him to dress up in old clothes and pose as a farmer.

This photograph shows the pair who posed for the painting. The woman on the left is Grant Wood's sister, Nan.

Elegant and refined, the portrait below shows newly-weds Mr and Mrs Andrews posing on their vast country estate. Although they are wearing lavish, fashionable clothes, the real emphasis is on the glowing English countryside.

Artist Thomas Gainsborough sometimes made little models to help him paint his landscapes, using mirrors for lakes and broccoli for trees.

Mr and Mrs Andrews
BY THOMAS GAINSBOROUGH, PAINTED IN ABOUT 1750

At the centre of the bustling picture below is a young Spanish princess, Margarita, surrounded by courtiers and servants – including the artist himself.

In the mirror on the wall, you can see a reflection of the king and queen under a red curtain. The royal couple must be standing opposite their reflection – in the same position as a viewer looking at the painting

Notice the young courtier trying to wake a dog with his foot.

The Family of Philip IV
BY DIEGO VELÁZQUEZ, PAINTED IN ABOUT 1656

This tense family portrait shows the artist's aunt, Laure, with her husband and two daughters.

The atmosphere seems strained and awkward. Laure's husband sits at a distance with his back to us, and no one is making eye contact with anyone.

Laure is wearing a black dress in mourning for her father, who had recently died. He appears in a picture frame beside her head.

Notice the family dog just running out of view.

The Bellelli Family
BY HILAIRE-GERMAIN-EDGAR DEGAS, PAINTED BETWEEN 1858–67

Portraits

These portraits are some of the most famous paintings ever made.
Although few of the sitters were well-known at the time they were painted,
their faces are now recognized all over the world.

This jolly-looking man turns to look at the viewer, as though he has been caught off guard. His upturned moustache and rosy cheeks give the impression that he is laughing.

The Laughing Cavalier
BY FRANS HALS, PAINTED IN 1624

The embroidered sleeves are full of beautiful detail – can you can spot any bees?

Many people think that the painting below is a portrait of the artist. He wears a red chaperon – a fashionable turban-like hat that wealthy gentlemen wore in medieval times.

The inscription at the bottom, in Latin, gives the name of the painter and the date: 'Jan van Eyck made me on 21 October 1433'.

Portrait of a Man (Self Portrait?)
BY JAN VAN EYCK, PAINTED IN 1433

The Mona Lisa is probably the most famous painting in the world. Nobody knows for sure who the portrait shows, but most experts think it is Lisa Gherardini, an Italian merchant's wife.

In 1911, the Mona Lisa was stolen from the Louvre – a huge museum in Paris – by a workman. It was discovered two years later in the thief's hotel room.

Leonardo da Vinci used a technique known as *sfumato* to blur the corners of her mouth and eyes. Her strange half-smile fascinates people, as it is so difficult to pin down. Is she happy, sad or simply bored?

Mona Lisa
BY LEONARDO DA VINCI, PAINTED IN ABOUT 1503–06

This is a self portrait by Mexican artist, Frida Kahlo. Around her neck she wears a hummingbird, a symbol of love and good fortune in Mexican culture. But prickly thorns are digging into her flesh, suggesting pain and suffering too.

Kahlo often included her pet monkeys and parrots in her self portraits.

The girl in the painting below is dressed in a strange, exotic costume. No-one knows who she was. The artist, Johannes Vermeer, used ultramarine blue – an expensive pigment made from semi-precious stones – to paint her rich blue headdress.

Self Portrait with Thorn Necklace and Hummingbird
BY FRIDA KAHLO, PAINTED IN 1940

Girl with a Pearl Earring
BY JOHANNES VERMEER, PAINTED IN 1665

When artist Jean-Auguste-Dominique Ingres was first asked to paint Madame Moitessier, he refused. He considered portrait painting a low form of art. But on meeting her, he found her so beautiful that he agreed. He left the picture unfinished for twelve years, before finally completing it in 1856.

Notice her reflection in the mirror behind.

Madame Moitessier's young daughter was supposed to be in the portrait too, but she had grown up by the time Ingres came to finish it.

The style of the dress changed more than once. The finished painting shows a glamorous silk dress embroidered with flowers.

Madame Moitessier
BY JEAN-AUGUSTE-DOMINIQUE INGRES, PAINTED IN 1856

Hidden meanings

This portrait of two powerful young men contains lots of objects with hidden meanings. It was painted about 500 years ago by Hans Holbein – one of the most famous portrait artists of his day.

The man on the right is Georges de Selve, who was 25 years old. His sombre outfit shows he is a man of the church – in fact he had just become a bishop.

The man on the left is Jean de Dinteville, then the French ambassador to Britain. Aged 29 at the time it was painted, he shows off his finest clothes, including a fur-trimmed cloak with padded shoulders.

The Ambassadors
BY HANS HOLBEIN THE YOUNGER, PAINTED IN 1533

1

What is the object by the men's feet? It's been distorted so you can only see it properly if you...

2

...shut one eye and look along one of the arrows.

3

If you look at it from the correct angle, you should be able to see a skull. It's there as a *memento mori*, a reminder that death comes to us all. But it's not all doom and gloom...

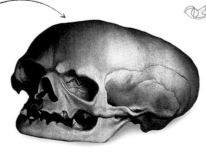

4

Hidden away in the top left-hand corner is a silver crucifix, to remind viewers of the Christian belief in an afterlife.

On the top shelf there are lots of different instruments. These were often used by seafarers to navigate at sea, and show off how well-travelled and knowledgeable the two men were.

The blue globe is a detailed map of the stars.

This instrument, known as a torquetum, was used to take and convert measurements.

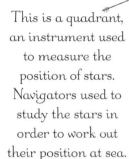

This is a quadrant, an instrument used to measure the position of stars. Navigators used to study the stars in order to work out their position at sea.

At the front are several kinds of instruments for measuring the angle of the sun, to give the exact time and date.

The lower shelf holds a globe and some musical instruments. The big stringed instrument is a lute – a symbol of harmony.

This globe has a detailed map of the world, including France.

Holbein made sure he marked Jean's hometown of Polisy.

If you look closely, you can see the lute has one broken string. The broken string – a symbol of discord – may be a reference to religious and political troubles of the time.

Holbein grew up in Germany, but moved to England to become court painter to King Henry VIII. In 1538-39, King Henry asked Holbein to paint several women, so he could choose one to marry. After seeing the portraits, Henry chose Anne of Cleves...

...but when he met her, he was disappointed and their marriage didn't last.

Anne of Cleves was painted in her best clothes, wearing a red velvet and gold dress embroidered with precious jewels.

Anne of Cleves
BY HANS HOLBEIN THE YOUNGER, PAINTED IN ABOUT 1539

Children

From wealthy princesses dressing to impress, to carefree children playing and having fun, these portraits capture very different kinds of childhood.

The Fife Player
BY EDOUARD MANET, PAINTED IN 1866

Manet may have based the boy on the left on his stepson, Leon Leenhoff. He wanted the boy to look 'firm, smooth and alive', so he used sharp colours to help him stand out from the flat background.

The painting's bright colours were inspired by French playing cards.

The picture includes a painted picture frame – making the girl look as if she was sitting in front of the painting.

A Young Princess
(Dorothea of Denmark?)
BY JAN GOSSAERT, PAINTED IN ABOUT 1530

This portrait probably shows Princess Dorothea of Denmark, who was about ten years old at the time. She wears a grown-up looking dress embroidered with hundreds of pearls, showing how wealthy and important she is.

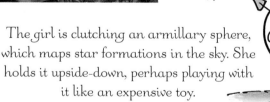

The girl is clutching an armillary sphere, which maps star formations in the sky. She holds it upside-down, perhaps playing with it like an expensive toy.

Lost in concentration, this boy is building a house of cards. The scene seems so still and quiet that the boy could be frozen in time. Notice how delicately the cards are balanced, as though a puff of wind could blow them over.

The House of Cards
BY JEAN-SIMÉON CHARDIN, PAINTED IN ABOUT 1736–37

These children look happy and content but, before the portrait was finished,
the baby on the left had died. Clues in the painting point to the baby's tragic future.

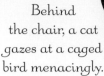

Behind
the chair, a cat
gazes at a caged
bird menacingly.

The eldest girl dangles two
cherries just out of the baby's
reach – representing the
youth he will never have.

In the corner,
a clock is decorated
with a cupid
holding a scythe.
This represents
death and the
passing of time.

The Graham Children
BY WILLIAM HOGARTH, PAINTED IN 1742

The baby is sitting on an elaborate
golden chair which could be
pulled along on wheels.

Surrounded by delicate flowers, these children are lighting paper
lanterns. American artist, John Singer Sargent, wanted to capture
the dreamy glow of twilight, so he only painted at dusk for a few
minutes at a time. It took him over a year to finish.

The warm, artificial glow
of the lanterns is reflected
on the girls' faces, hands
and pale white dresses.

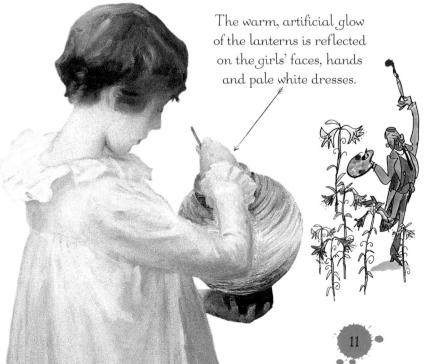

Carnation, Lily, Lily, Rose
BY JOHN SINGER SARGENT, PAINTED IN 1885–86

Sargent's friends teased him so much for his
extreme attention to detail, that he started to
call the painting 'Darnation, Silly, Silly, Pose'.

The great outdoors

Artists have painted landscapes in many different ways. Some painted what they saw, while others invented vast, atmospheric scenes of their own.

This calm country scene shows two men driving a horse-drawn cart – known as a 'wain' – across a shallow stream. The cart is empty, ready to be filled with hay. In the far distance, a group of farm labourers are hard at work, cutting down the hay with scythes.

The Hay Wain
BY JOHN CONSTABLE, PAINTED IN 1821

Notice how the red harnesses of the horses stand out from the background.

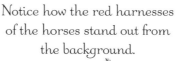

The artist John Constable was fascinated by cloudy skies, and he spent months making scientific studies of cloud formations. He described clouds as the 'keynote' of a painting.

At the bottom of *The Hay Wain*, a dog watches the horses with interest.

Constable noted the exact time and location on the back of his cloud studies.

Clouds
BY JOHN CONSTABLE, PAINTED IN 1822

In *The Avenue at Middelharnis*, rows of tall, thin trees lead your eye into the distance, giving the landscape a feeling of depth. Beyond the trees, you can see a village and a church with a tower.

The Avenue at Middelharnis
BY MEINDERT HOBBEMA, PAINTED IN 1689

This picture shows a dramatic night sky with swirling clouds and twinkling stars. A tall tree twists upwards like a burning flame. The thick, sweeping brushstrokes fill the scene with a feeling of movement.

It often seems to me that the night is much more alive and richly coloured than the day.

Van Gogh liked to use bright colours, often straight from the tube.

The Starry Night
BY VINCENT VAN GOGH, PAINTED IN 1889

Monet painted this picture on the beach, during his honeymoon in northern France. The woman on the left is probably his wife, Camille. He painted it fast, in one sitting, so the brushstrokes are loose and sketchy.

If you look closely, tiny grains of sand from the beach are trapped in the paint.

The Beach at Trouville
BY CLAUDE-OSCAR MONET, PAINTED IN 1870

French artist Paul Gauguin used his imagination to paint this exotic scene, while he was staying in Tahiti. He used flat, smooth shapes and vivid colours to create his idea of a perfect landscape, where people live in harmony with nature.

Notice a statue of a Tahitian moon goddess in the background.

Arearea
BY PAUL GAUGUIN, PAINTED IN 1892

Towns and cities

These paintings capture the hustle and bustle of urban life.

The painting below shows a boat race in Venice during carnival time. Lots of people are wearing festive carnival costumes. Venetian painter Canaletto was famous for painting scenes of Venice for wealthy tourists during the 18th century, and his cityscapes even became popular with royalty.

Most of the boats in the picture are gondolas – canal boats which are rowed along with one oar.

Venice: A Regatta on the Grand Canal
BY CANALETTO, PAINTED IN ABOUT 1735

Artist James Whistler named the painting below after a nocturne – a piece of music inspired by the night. He used soft, muted colours to give the misty London riverside a magical glow.

Many viewers were horrified by Whistler's loose, sketchy style. One well-known art critic, named John Ruskin, famously accused Whistler of...

...flinging a pot of paint in the public's face.

Nocturne: Blue and Gold - Old Battersea Bridge
BY JAMES ABBOTT McNEILL WHISTLER, PAINTED BETWEEN 1872–75

This New York scene shows the Radiator Building – a 22-storey skyscraper built in 1924. It has been transformed into a grid of white windows and sharp lines, without a person in sight.

Radiator Building - Night, New York
BY GEORGIA O'KEEFFE, PAINTED IN 1927

14

In *Nighthawks*, harsh yellow light streams out of a late-night diner, creating an eerie atmosphere in the empty street. The artist, Edward Hopper, was famous for using strong, moody lighting. The widescreen format makes it look like a scene from a film.

Nighthawks are nocturnal birds, and a nickname for people who do things at night, like the people in this scene.

Nighthawks
BY EDWARD HOPPER, PAINTED IN 1942

The artist and his wife, Jo, posed as the man and woman sitting at the counter.

Camille Pissarro painted this rainy Paris boulevard from a hotel window. He used broken brush strokes to show the way the light reflected off the wet street.

The Boulevard Montmartre at Night
BY CAMILLE PISSARRO, PAINTED IN 1897

The picture below shows a busy fair at Daisy Nook, a country park in northern England. During the early 20th century, northern England was full of industrial towns. Notice the tall factory chimney in the distance.

See if you can spot some children holding flags, balloons and toy windmills, and a queue of people waiting for a turn on a fairground ride called 'Thriller'.

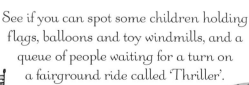

Lancashire Fair: Good Friday, Daisy Nook
BY LAURENCE STEPHEN LOWRY, PAINTED IN 1946

15

Daily life

These paintings show people doing everyday activities – from carrying out domestic chores to working hard earning a living.

Bright colours and swirling patterns surround this maid as she sets a dining table with fruit. Notice how the curved shapes of the patterned tablecloth and walls are echoed by the fruit, flowers and trees.

The picture below shows the cleanly swept courtyard of a house in Delft, a town in Holland.

The Red Room (Harmony in Red)
BY HENRI MATISSE, PAINTED IN 1908

The Courtyard of a House in Delft
BY PIETER DE HOOCH, PAINTED IN 1658

← A passage through the open door reveals the street beyond, giving the painting a sense of depth.

In the picture on the right, people on a busy street in Paris are hurrying through the rain. A little girl holds a hoop and stick – an old-fashioned game that was popular during the 19th century.

Renoir repainted the woman on the left a few years after he'd finished the rest of the picture. Her face is painted with smoother, more definite brushstrokes, and her dress has been updated to a plainer style.

The Umbrellas
BY PIERRE-AUGUSTE RENOIR,
PAINTED IN ABOUT 1881–86

16

Almost a hundred figures are packed onto this busy station platform. Trains were a very new mode of transport in the 1860s, which may be why the artist decided to make a picture about a train station. He was so determined to get every detail right, he employed an architect to paint the pillars and arches of the station roof.

A bride and groom hug their guests goodbye on the platform.

The Railway Station
BY WILLIAM POWELL FRITH, PAINTED IN 1862

A soldier in uniform is lifting a child into the air.

The two men on the right wearing top hats were famous Scotland Yard detectives. They are arresting someone trying to board the train.

The painting shows Paddington Station in London.

Can you spot a gamekeeper with his two hunting dogs?

A photographer took pictures of a real steam engine, to help the artist with his painting.

The painting on the right shows a vast field, where three peasant women are gathering up stray ears of wheat after a harvest. It's tiring work without much reward. Their small handfuls of wheat contrast with the huge, golden piles of grain behind them.

In the distance, a man on a horse is watching over the women. He's probably employed by the landowner to supervise their work.

The Gleaners
BY JEAN-FRANÇOIS MILLET, PAINTED IN 1857

Showtime

From circuses and nightclubs to ballets and plays, these paintings reveal the spectacle and drama of the performing world. And for some artists, the audience proved just as intriguing as the performances themselves.

Many of the details in this painting have been copied from an actual circus poster, which the artist would have seen plastered up around Paris. It's made up of thousands of individual coloured dots, although from a distance they seem to blend together.

This acrobat is somersaulting through the air.

Notice that there is no black in the painting – the dark areas are made up of blue dots.

The man in the front row wearing a top hat is probably Charles Angrand, one of the artist's friends.

Circus
BY GEORGES SEURAT, PAINTED IN 1890–91

Over a thousand copies of the poster on the right were printed to advertise a famous nightclub in Paris, called the *Moulin Rouge*. They made the artist famous overnight. His posters became so popular, they were often stolen as soon as they were put up.

Two dancers perform a style of dance known as a can-can under a spotlight. The male dancer was known as 'Valentin the Boneless' because he was so flexible.

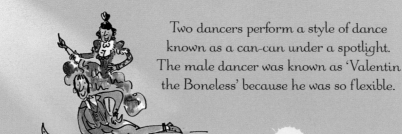

Moulin Rouge: La Goulue
BY HENRI DE TOULOUSE-LAUTREC, MADE IN 1891

Czech artist Alphonse Mucha designed the poster on the left to advertise a play at a theatre in Paris. The poster shows the play's leading lady, Sarah Bernhardt. Her sad expression and the pale, delicate colours reflect the play's tragic story.

Poster for 'La Dame aux Camélias'
BY ALPHONSE MUCHA, MADE IN 1896

At the Theatre shows a young girl leaning forward to see the stage, clasping her bouquet of flowers in excitement.

Notice the shimmering gold highlights around her face.

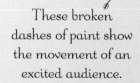

These broken dashes of paint show the movement of an excited audience.

At the Theatre
BY PIERRE-AUGUSTE RENOIR, PAINTED IN 1876–77

Edgar Degas was famous for his pictures of ballerinas. The pastel sketch below shows four young dancers warming up under the bright lights of the Paris Opera House. Their faces are blurry, making the drawing look as if it's been sketched hastily on the spot.

Degas was influenced by photography, which had recently been invented. The dancers have been cut off by the edge of the picture, as though this were a snapshot rather than a carefully constructed drawing. Degas dabbled in photography using an early camera.

There were so many young child dancers at the Paris Opera House, that they became known as 'the little rats'.

Blue Dancers
BY HILAIRE-GERMAIN-EDGAR DEGAS, DRAWN IN AROUND 1898

Nightlife

This painting, by famous artist Edouard Manet, offers a glittering glimpse into a famous French nightclub – the *Folies-Bergère*. The picture is packed full of details that capture the fashionable world of 19th-century Paris.

A barmaid looks out from behind the bar, waiting to serve her customer. The scene is cleverly arranged so you can see most of it in the mirror behind her – including one of the club's circus acts.

A Bar at the Folies-Bergère
BY EDOUARD MANET, PAINTED IN 1881–82

Notice the green boots in the top left corner. It's a reflection of an acrobat on a trapeze, high above the crowd.

Among the audience, you can just make out two elegantly dressed women. These are portraits of Manet's friends.

Some of the reflections don't match up. In the mirror, a man in a top hat is standing directly in front of the barmaid. It's where you, the viewer ought to be, as if you've been turned into the gentleman in the scene.

Manet signed his name on the label of a beer bottle.

One woman is watching the show through a pair of opera glasses.

The poster on the right shows the layout of the *Folies-Bergère*.
The bar in the painting was on the balcony opposite the stage – almost
level with the chandeliers, which you can see reflected in the mirror.
The club was famous for its dancing girls.

All kinds of exotic shows were
staged at the *Folies-Bergère* – even
a boxing kangaroo that could
fight a grown man.

TOUS LES SOIRS A 8 HEURES

32 RUE RICHER

FOLIES BERGÈRE

PRIMO de VOLTIGE-BALLETS

PANTOMIMES-OPÉRETTES

O. MÉTRA
ET
SON ORCHESTRE

PRIX UNIQUE 2ᶠ à toutes places non-louées

IMP. J. CHÉRET, 18, R. BRUNEL, PARIS.

Poster for the Folies-Bergère
BY JULES CHÉRET, MADE IN 1875

The barmaid
looks distracted,
and perhaps a bit
sad. Most people
who worked at the
nightclub were
underpaid and
overworked.

Manet painted several oil sketches like this one before
he completed the final version in his studio. Notice how he
changed the position of the barmaid and her reflection
in the final painting.

Oil Sketch for
'A Bar at the Folies-Bergère'
BY EDOUARD MANET, PAINTED BETWEEN 1881–82

Emotions

Some of the most famous paintings have been inspired by strong emotions, from sadness and grief to happiness and love. The artists probably intended you to feel those emotions when you looked at them.

In the Car
BY ROY LICHTENSTEIN, PAINTED IN 1963

American artist Roy Lichtenstein based *In the Car* on a comic book series called *Girls' Romances*. It suggests a tense, dramatic moment between a man and woman in a car.

Lichtenstein even copied the dotty effect used in some cheap printed comics, by painting through a metal screen punctured with tiny holes.

Van Gogh painted these bright sunflowers to decorate his friend's room, who was coming to stay with him at his house in the south of France. Van Gogh believed that yellow was the colour of happiness and friendship.

The Scream
BY EDVARD MUNCH, PAINTED IN 1895

The haggard figure in the painting on the left is standing beneath a swirling, blood-red sky, clutching its head in pain.

Some people think that the figure's skull-like face was based upon an ancient mummy.

Munch was inspired by watching a sunset turn the sky red and suddenly feeling an overwhelming feeling of anxiety.

Sunflowers
BY VINCENT VAN GOGH, PAINTED IN 1888

I sensed an infinite scream passing through nature.

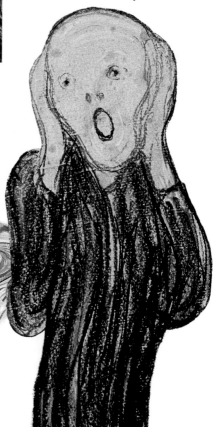

Picasso's girlfriend, Dora Maar, posed for this painting soon after civil war tore Spain apart. Her weeping face represents the suffering of war. Picasso painted her from two different angles. So, although both eyes gaze out at us, we are looking at her face from the side. The jagged, distorted features intensify the emotion in the picture.

The glittering, golden image below shows a couple kissing. They are surrounded by decorative, swirling patterns that seem to overlap and mingle, symbolising their togetherness.

Dora Maar's oval fingernails look like tears rolling down her face.

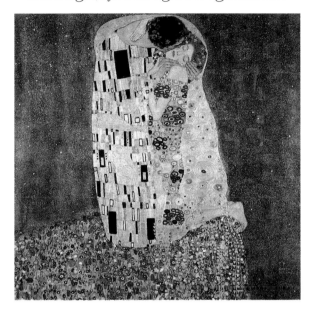

The Kiss

BY GUSTAV KLIMT, PAINTED BETWEEN 1907–08

Weeping Woman

BY PABLO PICASSO, PAINTED IN 1937

Austrian artist Gustav Klimt was interested in fashion design, and many of his paintings show people wearing beautiful patterned fabric. He designed his own work clothes too – a long, colourful robe and sandals.

Klimt used paper-thin pieces of gold and silver leaf to decorate his picture. He scraped curls on top of the gold, which shimmers in the light.

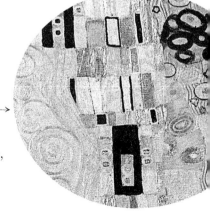

Ophelia is based on a scene from one of Shakespeare's most famous plays, *Hamlet*. In the play, Ophelia drowns in a stream while picking flowers, having been driven mad by grief.

To paint Ophelia, the artist had a model lie fully clothed in a bathtub for hours on end. She lay there so long, she caught a terrible cold.

All the flowers in the picture have symbolic meanings. Poppies represent death, while daisies stand for beauty and innocence.

Ophelia

BY JOHN EVERETT MILLAIS, PAINTED IN 1851–52

Weather

From heavy rainstorms and snow to bright sunny spells,
these paintings capture all kinds of different weather.

Netherlandish painter Hendrick Avercamp was famous for
painting snowy winter scenes of Kampen, the city where he lived.
Known as the 'Mute of Kampen', he was unable to hear or speak.

A *Winter Scene* is full of
carefully observed details
of people having fun on
a frozen lake.

This elegantly dressed
man and woman are
skating across the river
hand in hand.

How many
birds can you
spot in the tree?

On the left,
some children are
throwing snowballs
at each other.

Look out for an unfortunate
pair slipping over on the ice.

A Winter Scene
with Skaters near a Castle
BY HENDRICK AVERCAMP, PAINTED IN ABOUT 1608–09

Many of the skaters wear
long cloaks and thick winter
hats to keep out the cold.

The whole scene, including the castle, was painted from
the artist's imagination, but it is filled with lifelike details.

These people are being
pulled across the ice on a
horse-drawn sleigh.

This 19th-century painting shows a steam train rushing over a railway bridge during a storm. The dramatic perspective, with the bridge angled towards us, makes the train appear to be zooming straight at us.

Trains were an exciting new invention, in contrast with the old road bridge just visible in the distance, and included here as a reminder of the past.

To prepare for the painting, Turner stuck his head out of a train window for ten minutes during a storm.

Rain, Steam, and Speed - The Great Western Railway
BY JOSEPH MALLORD WILLIAM TURNER, PAINTED IN 1844

Waterloo Bridge
BY ANDRÉ DERAIN, PAINTED IN 1906

The picture on the left shows a dazzling river scene. The artist, André Derain, used blazing golds and pinks to show the sunlight above the cool, quiet waters. He didn't want to weaken the bright colours by blending them together, so he applied thick brushstrokes of pure colour.

Also known as *The Great Wave*, this famous Japanese print shows a huge wave about to crash over three tiny boats. From this angle, even the peak of Mount Fuji is dwarfed by the enormous wave.

Under the Wave, off Kanagawa
BY KATSUSHIKA HOKUSAI, MADE BETWEEN ABOUT 1830–32

If you look closely, the curls of white foam look like menacing claws.

Thousands of copies of the print were made using carved wooden blocks. The blocks were coated with ink, and paper was pressed onto them to create each finished print.

Myths and stories

These dramatic pictures were inspired
by famous myths and stories.

The painting below tells the story of Saint George and the dragon.
A dragon had been terrorising a town, and each day it demanded a
maiden to eat. One day, a beautiful princess was chosen, but George
came to the rescue and defeated the dragon.

The dragon
is roaring in pain
after being struck
by George's lance.

In the story,
the princess tied
her belt around the
dragon's neck and led
it back to the town.

Saint George and the Dragon
BY PAOLO UCCELLO, PAINTED IN ABOUT 1470

The swirl gathering in the sky represents
the eye of God, helping George to victory.

Inspired by an ancient myth, *Bacchus
and Ariadne* captures the moment
when Bacchus, Greek god of wine, falls
in love with Princess Ariadne. Ariadne
has just been abandoned on an island.
On seeing her, Bacchus leaps towards
her from his chariot.

Beside Bacchus is
a half-boy, half-goat
called a satyr.

Bacchus and Ariadne
BY TITIAN, PAINTED IN 1520–23

The painting was
commissioned by a wealthy
duke. Titian probably based
these cheetahs on ones
he saw in the duke's
private zoo.

26

King Cophetua and the Beggar Maid is a medieval legend that tells the story of an African king who fell in love with a beggar named Penelophon. Notice how the beggar maid in the painting is wearing a plain dress with bare feet, contrasting with the finery around her.

The picture on the right illustrates the Greek myth of Icarus. In the story, Icarus tried to escape from a tower using wings made out of feathers and wax. He flew too close to the sun, melting the wax, and fell into the sea and drowned.

Icarus is part of a series of pictures made for the book 'Jazz', written and illustrated by the artist Henri Matisse. Each shape in the picture was cut out of paper - a technique Matisse called 'drawing with scissors'.

Icarus

PLATE VIII FROM THE ILLUSTRATED BOOK, 'JAZZ'.
BY HENRI MATISSE, MADE IN 1947

King Cophetua
and the Beggar Maid
BY SIR EDWARD BURNE-JONES, PAINTED IN 1884

Below is another painting inspired by Icarus. In the bottom right-hand corner, you can just see the ends of Icarus's legs, as he falls into the sea. In the foreground, farm labourers carry on with their work, unaffected by the drama behind them.

Landscape with the Fall of Icarus

UNKNOWN, AFTER PIETER BRUEGEL, PAINTED IN ABOUT 1558

A large ship sails past, drawing your attention away from Icarus.

Springtime

This painting used to hang in one of the palaces of the powerful Medici family in Florence, Italy. It is a celebration of love, new beginnings and spring, and was probably painted as a wedding gift.

The picture is full of characters from ancient myths, watched over by Venus, the Roman goddess of love, in the middle.

Mercury was the messenger of the gods. He seems to be pushing away a rain cloud with his staff. Notice his winged sandals...

According to myth, these sandals allowed him to fly through the sky.

Allegory of Spring
(OR, IN ITALIAN, PRIMAVERA)
BY SANDRO BOTTICELLI, PAINTED IN 1477–82

These dancers – known as the Three Graces – represent grace and beauty.

The three Graces look very similar. Some people think they may be based on an Italian beauty named Simonetta Vespucci. The artist Sandro Botticelli so admired Simonetta, he asked to be buried at her feet.

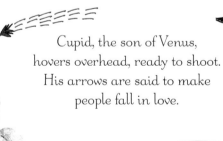

Cupid, the son of Venus, hovers overhead, ready to shoot. His arrows are said to make people fall in love.

A dark halo of leaves makes Venus stand out clearly.

More than 500 different plants and flowers are shown in the garden. The orange trees in the background were a symbol of the Medici family who owned the painting.

The strange, blue-winged figure is Zephyrus, the wind of Spring. His puffed-up cheeks and billowing robes are meant to suggest the wind blowing. He is reaching out to a shy-looking nymph – in myth, a type of nature spirit. Notice the flowers dropping from her lips – according to myth, this happened when she spoke.

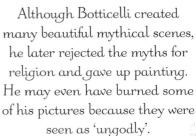

At the touch of Zephyrus, the nymph is transformed into a beautiful goddess – Flora, goddess of flowers and spring, who steps forward, scattering roses.

The *Allegory of Spring* is a huge painting – in real life, it fills a whole wall. It was created with a kind of paint known as egg tempera, which gives very strong colours. But egg tempera also dries very fast. So Botticelli had to paint quickly, and could only work on a small section at a time.

Egg tempera is made by blending coloured powders, or pigments, with egg yolk.

Presumed Self Portrait
(DETAIL FROM *THE ADORATION OF THE MAGI*)
BY SANDRO BOTTICELLI, PAINTED IN 1475

Although Botticelli created many beautiful mythical scenes, he later rejected the myths for religion and gave up painting. He may even have burned some of his pictures because they were seen as 'ungodly'.

Shapes and colours

Many of these bold, bright pictures look like unusual patterns or colourful designs. Paintings don't have to be about recognizable people or places – they can just show arrangements of shapes or colours.

French artist Sonia Delaunay based this picture on the patterns of light produced by an electric street lamp. She used circular shapes to capture the 'halo of moving colours' that she saw around the lamp.

Delaunay said colour was the 'skin of the world', and wanted to apply her art to everything around her. The photograph below shows two models wearing her designs. She even painted the car.

Electric Prisms
BY SONIA DELAUNAY, MADE IN 1914

Electric street lights were a new invention at the time, and had recently been installed on the streets of Paris.

The painting on the right is rather like a pattern of coloured blocks. Artist Paul Klee associated each colour with a different musical note. He believed that arranging colours together was like arranging notes in a melody.

Look carefully – can you see the roofs and turrets of a castle?

Castle and Sun
BY PAUL KLEE, PAINTED IN 1928

Composition VII is made up of lots of coloured shapes and squiggly lines. The shapes look as if they are swirling around, as if caught in a violent storm.

It is part of a series of ten 'compositions' inspired by stories from the Bible, including the Great Flood. As he was painting, the artist repeated the word flood over and over again.

Composition VII
BY WASSILY KANDINSKY, PAINTED IN 1913

The picture below is inspired by Shakespeare's tragic play, *Hamlet*. Notice the outline of the face of Ophelia – a character from the play who drowned while picking flowers by a stream. The loose, smudgy shapes and hazy colours make this picture feel like an image of a dream.

Mark Rothko painted huge canvases with big shapes, so that the viewer could feel lost inside them. These soft, blurry blocks of colour seem to meet in the middle to create a glowing horizon.

Ophelia among the Flowers
BY ODILON REDON, PAINTED IN ABOUT 1905–08

Even the flowers look strange and unrecognizable, as if painted from a distant memory. »

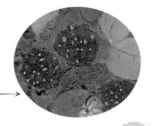

Orange and Yellow
BY MARK ROTHKO, PAINTED IN 1956

Index